HELP, HOPE AND HEALING
for Haiti

We Endure, We Survive, We Live and
Celebrate God's Grace

HELP, HOPE AND HEALING for Haiti

We Endure, We Survive, We Live and Celebrate God's Grace

Whitman Publishing, LLC
PUBLISHING SINCE 1934
whitmanbooks.com
3101 Clairmont Road • Suite G • Atlanta GA 30329

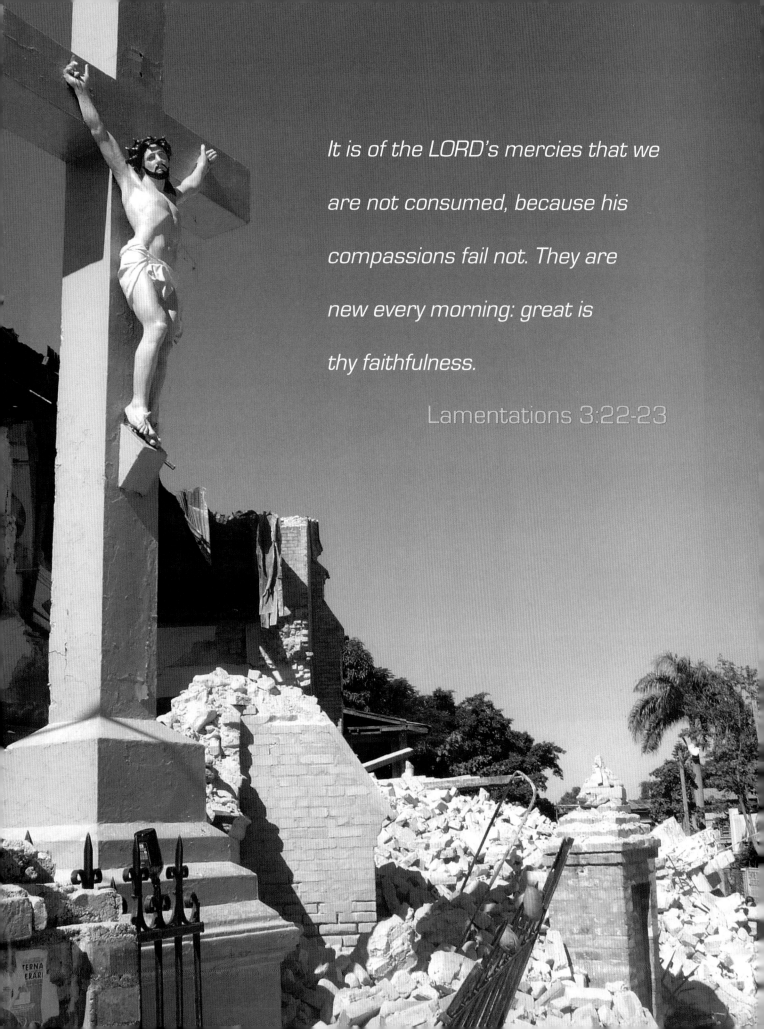

It is of the LORD's mercies that we are not consumed, because his compassions fail not. They are new every morning: great is thy faithfulness.

Lamentations 3:22-23

Rising From The Ruins

After defeating Napoleon's elite army with its own army of slaves, Haiti shook the world by becoming the first republic led by the black race. Shunned by the international community for over a century, it struggled from birth. Despite a rich culture and people made strong by adversity, it suffered at the hands of some of its own countrymen, who used political office to satisfy their own thirst for power and wealth.

But more recently, things were improving. Through slow and steady progress, foreign investors were looking to Haiti. Tensions within the country eased; the rule of law and order became more established. Until January 12, 2010.

Communities in southern Haiti crumbled as a long-dormant fault line suddenly unleashed a massive earthquake. Some lives ended immediately as buildings collapsed. Others struggled for life only to lose the battle. But here and there, miracles broke through the shattered brick: a toddler, an old woman, a few shoppers in a supermarket. More and more emerged until more than 130 had been resurrected from certain death.

More miraculous is the spirit of the Haitian community. Although countless churches have fallen apart, the faith of the people remains firm. In the tent cities, there was the sound of weeping, but at night — lilting through the air — came the songs of faith, Christian faith that believes and believes and believes again despite any evidence to the contrary.

The miracles were not confined to Haiti, though. People who could not find Haiti on a map opened their hearts and gave. From a small boy raising money by riding his bike, to famous stars with household names, there was a worldwide response with one goal — help Haiti.

Still others rushed to help in person. Rescue crews came from countries near and far, working beside Haitians whose bare hands were bloodied from digging, helping to save those buried alive. The United States and Canadian military arrived, working beside an injured United Nations peacekeeping force, not to invade or destroy but to save and to heal. Medical teams operated in 19th century conditions to salvage a limb, to save a life. Sometimes the two choices were mutually exclusive, but always the welfare of the injured prevailed.

Organizations such as The Salvation Army mobilized from their own crushed buildings to rush aid. The Haitians came to them seeking desperately needed help, knowing despite the rubble that remained of The Salvation Army in Haiti, hope could be found there. They were not disappointed.

Yes, the earthquake leveled a country. But the miracles rose from the ruins.

— Major Allen Satterlee,
Salvation Army Divisional Commander, Western Jamaica Division

(Above) A father carries his daughter after a major earthquake on January 12, 2010, in Port-au-Prince, Haiti. (Opposite page) This image obtained from Twitter purportedly shows Haitians standing amid rubble on January 12, 2010, in Port-au-Prince after a huge quake measuring 7.0 rocked the impoverished Caribbean nation of Haiti.

But they that wait upon the LORD shall renew their strength; they shall mount up with wings as eagles; they shall run, and not be weary; and they shall walk, and not faint.

Isaiah 40:31

"This is a tragic situation and we will work alongside the Haitian government to provide immediate assistance in the rescue effort. On behalf of the American people, I wish to convey our sympathy, thoughts and prayers to the people of Haiti who have been affected by this devastating earthquake."

USAID Administrator Rajiv Shah

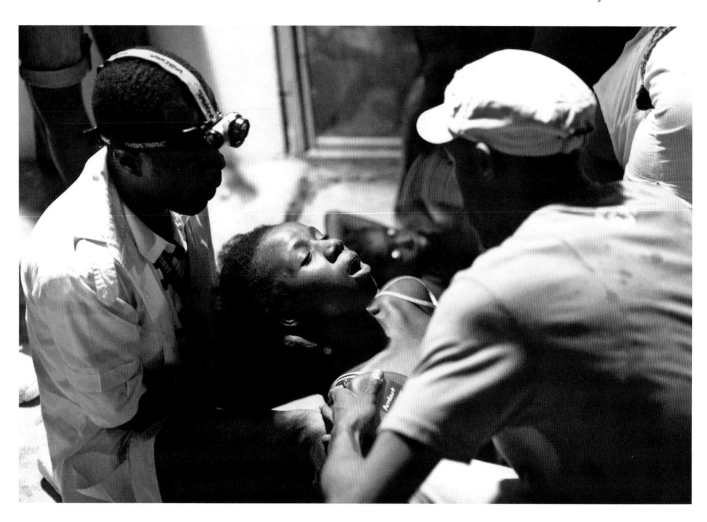

(Above) A man tries to talk on a cell phone on January 12, 2010, in Port-au-Prince, Haiti. A 7.0 earthquake rocked Haiti, followed by at least a dozen aftershocks, causing widespread devastation in the capital of Port-au-Prince. (Opposite page) A woman faints in the arms of a medic in an emergency clinic in Petionville.

(Above) An injured person is carried on a stretcher after the earthquake. (Opposite page) Gregor Avril, the executive director of the Haitian Association of Industry, helps an injured child with the support of artist/musician Mikaben.

"Where men, women and children are suffering under the heaviest of burdens, that place must, for that moment, become the center of our world's attention, the world's compassion and the world's humanitarian help."

British Prime Minister Gordon Brown

I will say of the LORD, He is my refuge and my fortress:

my God; in him will I trust.

Psalm 91:2

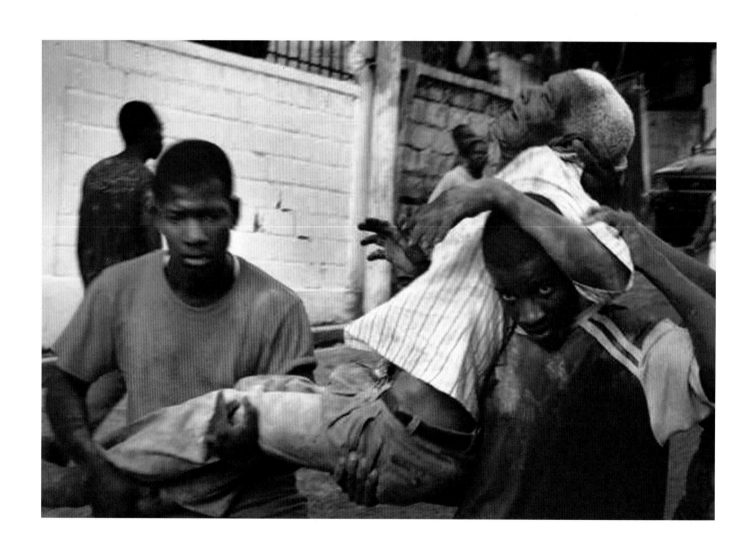

(Above) People pass by the remains of a six-story communication building. (Opposite page) A man being helped following the powerful 7.0 quake that struck Port-au-Prince. A vast international aid effort swung into action as a devastated President Rene Preval appealed for help.

(Above) Residents of Port-au-Prince stare through the fence at the ruins of the presidential palace, the official residence of Haitian President Rene Preval. (Opposite page) An injured girl is given water by a French aid worker at a makeshift field hospital.

"We will keep the victims and their families in our prayers.

We will be resolute in our response, and I pledge to the people of

Haiti that you will have a friend and partner in the United States of

America today and going forward."

U.S. President Barack Obama

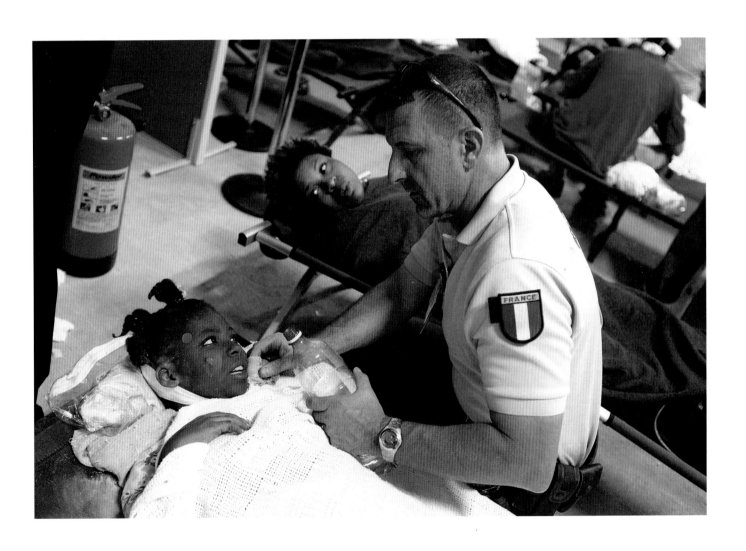

❝ The Haitian tragedy surpasses any that we have suffered. **❞**

Mexican President Felipe Calderon

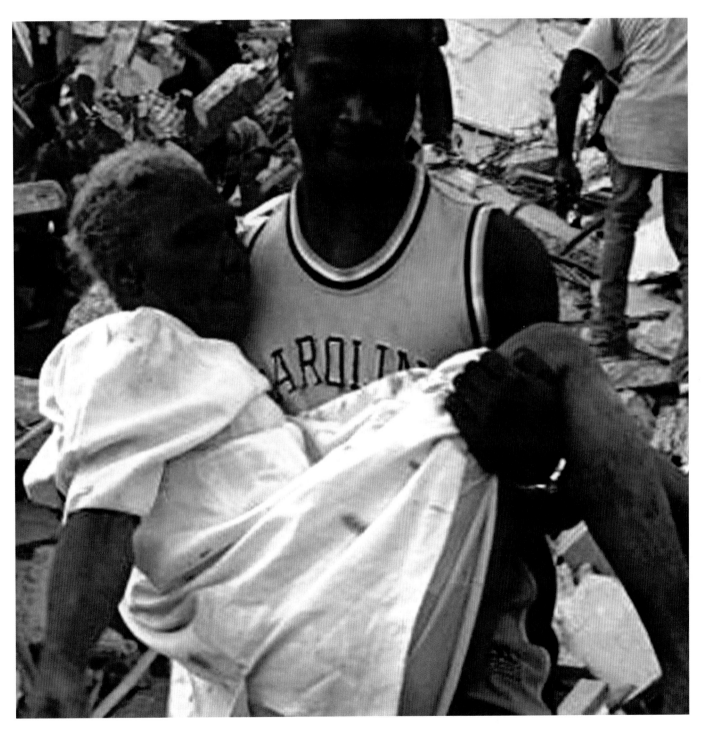

(Above) Injured are carried through the rubble. (Opposite page) Haitian President Rene Preval (center) along with his wife, Elisabeth Débrosse Delatour, meet with Dr. Barth Green, chairman of the Department of Neurosurgery at the University of Miami, as he brings a team of doctors to help with disaster victims on January 13, 2010, in Port-au-Prince, Haiti.

(Above) Debris litters a street on January 13, 2010, in Port-au-Prince. (Opposite page) Local residents wander amidst the ruins of their hometown hours after the earthquake. More than 100,000 people were feared dead after the calamitous earthquake razed homes, hotels and hospitals, leaving the capital in ruins and bodies strewn in the streets.

“The United States will help Haitians rebuild their vibrant country. It is encouraging to see the outpouring of aid to Haiti from the United States and around the world and we offer our full support to all involved in the relief process. Haiti will need our support today, tomorrow, and in the years to come.**”**

John Kerry, U.S. Senate Foreign
Relations Committee chairman

“ This is a time when we are reminded of the common humanity that we all share. With just a few hundred miles of ocean between us and a long history that binds us together, Haitians are neighbors of the Americas and here at home. So we have to be there for them in their hour of need. **”**

U.S. President Barack Obama

(Above) An injured women and her baby are seen at a makeshift field hospital. (Opposite page) U.S. President Barack Obama makes a statement on the Haitian earthquake with Vice President Joe Biden at the White House in Washington, D.C., January 13, 2010.

(Above) Rescue workers unload medical and other relief supplies flown in on a Venezuelan military cargo plane January 13, 2010, in Port-au-Prince. (Opposite page) Haitians pass destroyed buildings on January 13, 2010.

"We have been surprised by this sad news ... We have not been able to have direct contact with our ambassador there or with the Haitian authorities. But immediately we are going to hold a meeting with the business leaders in Haiti."

Nicolas Maduro, Venezuelan Foreign Minister

❝I saw American Red Cross staff, armed with first aid kits, going out to treat people. They have a truck and a door that they were using as a stretcher, and they were taking injured to a field hospital run by another country's Red Cross. And every time a Red Cross truck would go through the streets, the people would clear the way to let it pass.**❞**

American Red Cross President and CEO Gail McGovern

(Above) People grieve together after a relative was killed in the massive earthquake. (Opposite page) Members of a 60-member Dutch search and rescue team at Eindhoven airport shortly before their departure for Haiti.

(Above) Sarlah Chand, 65, is relieved as search and rescue workers tend to her after they rescued her from under the rubble of what is left of the Hotel Montana more than 50 hours after the massive earthquake destroyed the hotel. (Opposite page) Rescuers carry a 3-month-old baby found alive following a powerful earthquake that left much of the capital city in ruins.

"I have said that we cannot talk about Haiti, a country which has suffered so many disasters over this year, as a country where we can only give a week's sympathy or a week's charity."

British Prime Minister Gordon Brown

❝I was saddened by what I saw and yet I saw the faces of the Haitians, who were calm and patient.**❞**

U.N. Secretary General Ban Ki-moon

(Above) Members of the Fairfax County Urban Search & Rescue Team in Virginia and a co-worker support earthquake survivor Tarmo Joveer on January 14, 2010, after he was freed from 40 hours in the rubble of the United Nations Stabilization Headquarters. (Opposite page) A member of the Fairfax County Urban Search & Rescue Team and her K-9 partner search the property for more survivors.

(Above) A young child lays on a stretcher as she gets medical care after the massive earthquake. (Opposite page) People wave at a helicopter in the center of Port-au-Prince, on January 14, 2010.

"This is a historic disaster. We have never been confronted with such a disaster in the U.N. memory. It is like no other.**"**

Elisabeth Byrs, spokeswoman for the U.N. Office
for the Coordination of Humanitarian Affairs

"Haitians are grieving, but they are also buoyed by the generous outpouring of support from around the world. Despite the losses they have suffered, they are working hard to turn the empty lots, golf courses and churchyards where they have taken refuge into places where they can live in dignity."

Mark Fried of Oxfam, a relief organization

(Above) People wait in line for water from the fire department after the earthquake.
(Opposite page) Dusk falls over a tent city of Haitians displaced by the earthquake.

(Above) Bolivian U.N. peacekeepers distribute water and meals to the residents in Cite Soleil.
(Opposite page) Wrecked buildings lie in a street of Port-au-Prince, January 15, 2010,
following the massive earthquake on January 12.

"Haiti needs the massive support of its partners in the international community in the medium and long term."

Haitian Prime Minister Jean-Max Bellerive

" It was unbelievable, but we were amazed to see medics from many nations and languages working together brilliantly to help the injured and distressed. "

Andy Hawthorne, director of The Message Trust

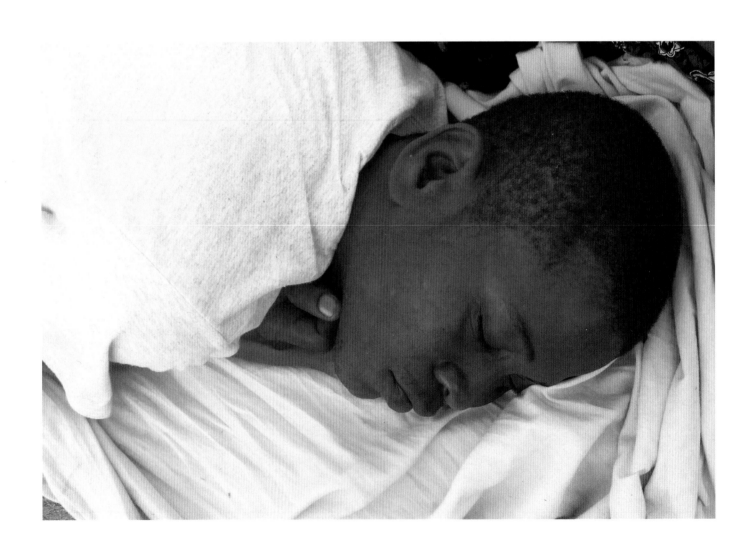

(Above) A Bolivian U.N. peacekeeper hands over a baby to his father during a distribution of water and meals to the residents in Cite Soleil, Port-au-Prince. (Opposite page) A young man catches some sleep in earthquake-ravaged Haiti.

(Above) A boy carries a bucket of water away from a broken water pipe in Cite Soleil after the earthquake. (Opposite page) Relief agencies distribute water as people use any means they have to carry it away.

" There's just an unbelievable spirit amongst the Haitian people. And while that earthquake destroyed a lot, it didn't destroy their spirit. "

Former U.S. President George W. Bush

"I never give up hope, no. We were praying a lot for this to happen. I called my dad (in Miami) to let him know, and he is very happy."

Maxime Janvier, whose mother was rescued from the ruins of a cathedral

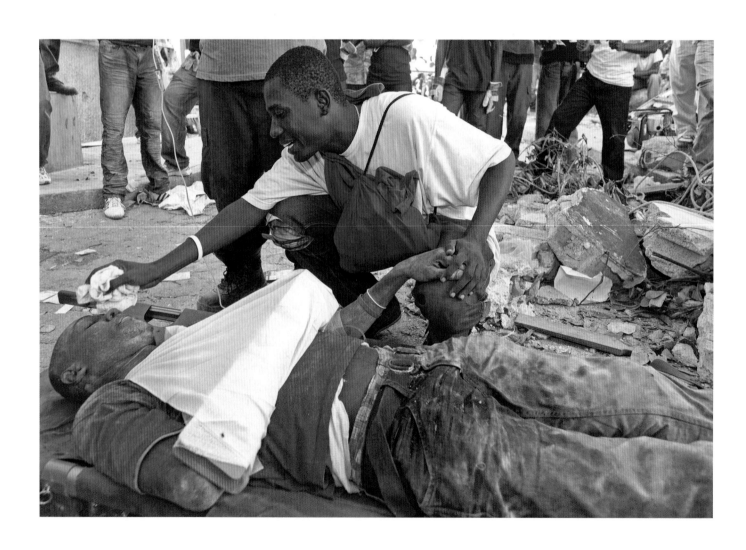

(Above) A statue of Jesus remains standing outside the ruins of Sacre Coeur Church in Port-au-Prince. (Opposite page) A friend comforts student Billy Clerge after 69 ½ hours under the rubble of University of Port au Prince after being dug out by the Fairfax County Urban Search & Rescue Team, part of USAID.

(Above) Women comfort one another after a church service at the Assembly of God. (Opposite page) Search and rescue workers from Mexico search for a way to reach survivors trapped under the rubble of what is left of the St. Gerard building after the massive earthquake. Children could be heard inside the building begging for help.

" In these extremely painful moments, my thoughts go to the Haitian people who are exhibiting great courage in the face of the implacable adversity of nature. **"**

French President Nicolas Sarkozy

"I know of the great resilience and strength of the Haitian people. You have been severely tested, but I believe that Haiti can come back even stronger and better in the future."

U.S. Secretary of State Hillary Clinton

(Above) U.S. Secretary of State Hillary Clinton meets with Haiti's President Rene Preval (left) to discuss conditions in the country. (Opposite page) Delmas stadium was transformed into a refugee camp following the quake.

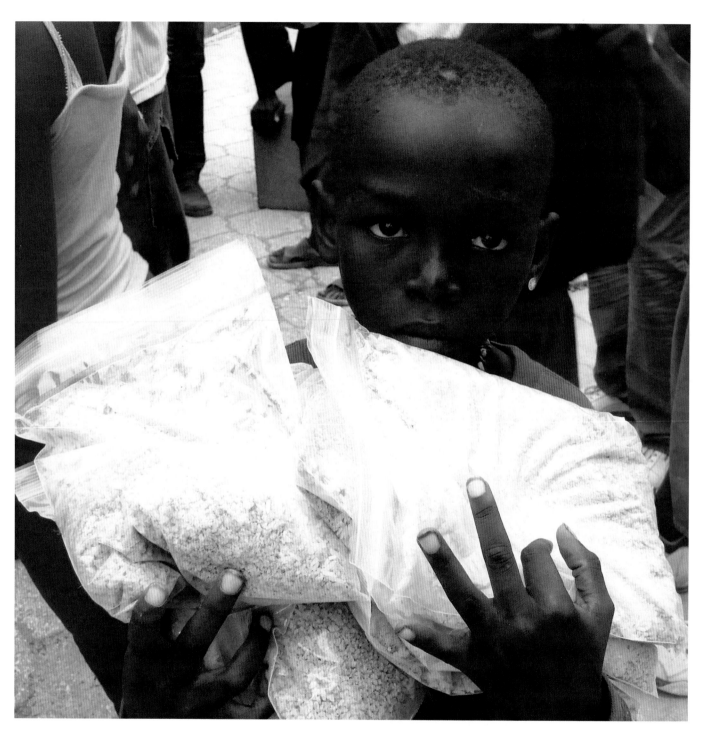

(Above) A young Haitian boy walks away from a Salvation Army supply line with an armload of rice. (Opposite page) President Barack Obama speaks as former President Bill Clinton and former President George W. Bush listen in the Rose Garden of the White House on January 16, 2010. Obama spoke about how the American people can help in the recovery and rebuilding effort in Haiti.

"You will not be forsaken, you will not be forgotten. In this, your hour of greatest need, America stands with you."

U.S. President Barack Obama

The LORD is my shepherd; I shall not want. He maketh me to lie down in green pastures: he leadeth me beside the still waters. He restoreth my soul: he leadeth me in the paths of righteousness for his name's sake. Yea, though I walk through the valley of the shadow of death, I will fear no evil: for thou art with me; thy rod and thy staff they comfort me. Thou preparest a table before me in the presence of mine enemies: thou anointest my head with oil; my cup runneth over. Surely goodness and mercy shall follow me all the days of my life: and I will dwell in the house of the LORD forever.

Psalm 23

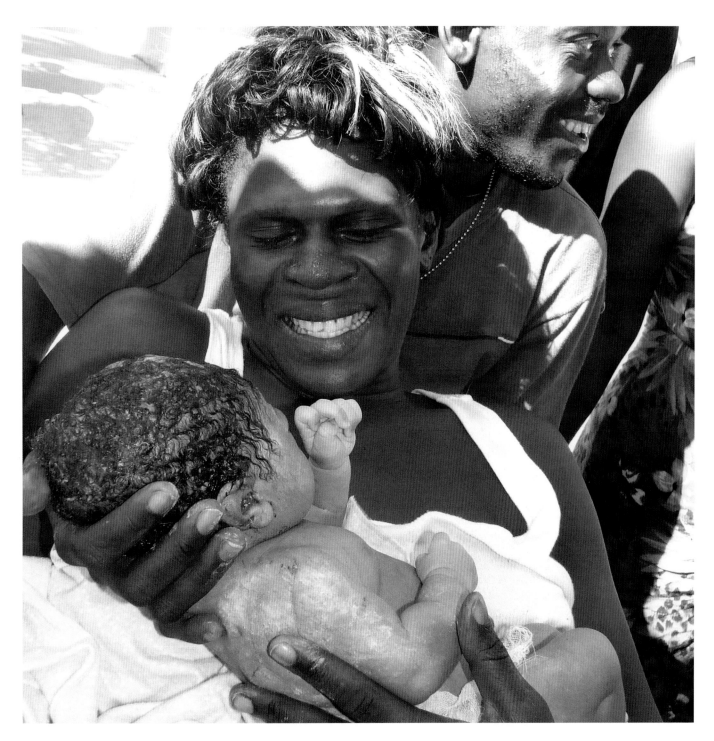

(Above) Even in disaster, there is life. A Haitian woman cradles her newborn baby, born just days after the devastating earthquake. (Opposite page) Residents of Port-au-Prince reach out for water distributed outside the Hospital Espoire by the humanitarian group Save the Children.

(Above) Women pray in the Cite Soleil's MSF center in Port-au-Prince.
(Opposite page) Injured people in the Cite Soleil's MSF center.

❝Haiti can become an example of what humanity can do for itself. In Haiti we have been asked how long the spirit of cooperation can last before egoism, chauvinism, mixed motives and contempt for other countries prevails.❞

Former Cuban President Fidel Castro

"You get to the playground areas and the kids are just playing. They're enjoying today; they're enjoying that moment, and that's how the Haitian people are. In the face of all of this, they've been singing and just praising God that they survived, and they are here and they will get through this."

Laurie Bickel, one of the administrators of God's Littlest Angels Orphanage

(Above) Boys play soccer at a refuge in Port-au-Prince on January 16, 2010. (Opposite page)
Two boys play with makeshift kites, made from trash bags, cloth and string.

(Above) Children are staying at the orphanage that was destroyed during the earthquake in Fontamara close to Port-au-Prince. (Opposite page) U.N. staff member Jens Christensen of Denmark being pulled from the rubble of the headquarters of the United Nations mission January 17, 2010.

"We rushed [a teenage girl buried in the rubble] to the Israeli hospital where she underwent surgery, and now, five days after the earthquake, she is in stable condition. Seeing this miraculous recovery and life saved before my eyes was one of the most profound moments of my life."

David Darg, of Operation Blessing International

"I'm a man of prayer, and I try to bring hope to people when I can. Some people may not have known before this that Haiti is less than 1,000 miles from the States. Haiti is a close neighbor, and we in this country need to remember that and help the people there rebuild."

Rev. Rodolphe Arty, a Haitian native and associate pastor at St. Thomas the Apostle Catholic Church in Naperville, Illinois

(Above) Haitian people pray during the Sunday mass organized by the priest outside of the destroyed cathedral of Port-au-Prince. (Opposite page) Mexican Federal Police rescuers look for survivors at the collapsed National Palace.

(Above) Former U.S. President Bill Clinton and Marc Mezvinsky, Chelsea Clinton's fiance, help unload a delivery of medical supplies at the Central Hospital. (Opposite page) Secretary General of the United Nations Ban Ki Moon shakes hands with U.S. rescuers during a visit to the destroyed headquarters of the MINUSTAH in Port-au-Prince.

"I believe before this earthquake, Haiti had the best chance in my lifetime to escape its history. I still believe that. The Haitians want to just amend their development plan to take account of what's happened in Port-au-Prince and west, figure out what they got to do about that, and then go back to implementing it. But it's going to take a lot of help and a long time."

Bill Clinton, former U.S. President and United Nations special envoy to Haiti

"The Haitian people have got a tough journey, yet it's amazing how terrible tragedies can bring out the best of the human spirit."

Former U.S. President George W. Bush

(Above) A man holds up a Haitian flag while standing in line for food rations at a tent city. Members of World Food Program distributed vitamin-enriched biscuits to Haitians while United Nations soldiers controlled the crowd. (Opposite page) Members of a Colombian search and rescue team signal what they hear as they listen on special devices for sounds of someone alive at a collapsed building at the Hotel Montana.

(Above) Members of the Los Angeles County Fire Department Search and Rescue Team rescue a Haitian woman from a collapsed building January 17, 2010, in Port-au-Prince. The woman had been trapped in the building for five days without food or water. (Opposite page) A young woman makes a phone call at one of four telecom centers set up by Télécoms Sans Frontières, a relief agency that offers free, reliable communication services during disasters.

"I asked God to free me, and I promised him I wouldn't waste my second chance."

Benito Revolus, rescued from the rubble of a hospital

"I want to send a message of hope because God is still with us even in the depths of this tragedy, and life is not over."

Rev. Henry Marie Landasse

(Above) Rescue workers climb over the rubble of a house, looking for people in the wreckage. (Opposite page) Knickknacks from a fallen shelf litter a table inside what was a cozy home.

(Above) Hundreds of people, some with U.S. passports, stand in a long line outside of the U.S. Embassy as they try to leave the country. (Opposite page) Haitians line up in front of the U.S. Embassy seeking visas.

"We stand alongside all the people in Haiti affected by this terrible disaster in prayer, thought and action as the situation unfolds. We pray for the rescue of those still trapped and look towards the rebuilding of lives and communities."

Rowan Williams, Archbishop of Canterbury

The first effort was to try to save human lives, and we did save a few at the hotel — my wife and some employees, by hand, dug out three survivors. But that part is over. Now, you know, we need to move on and rebuild.

Alain Villard, T-shirt factory and hotel owner

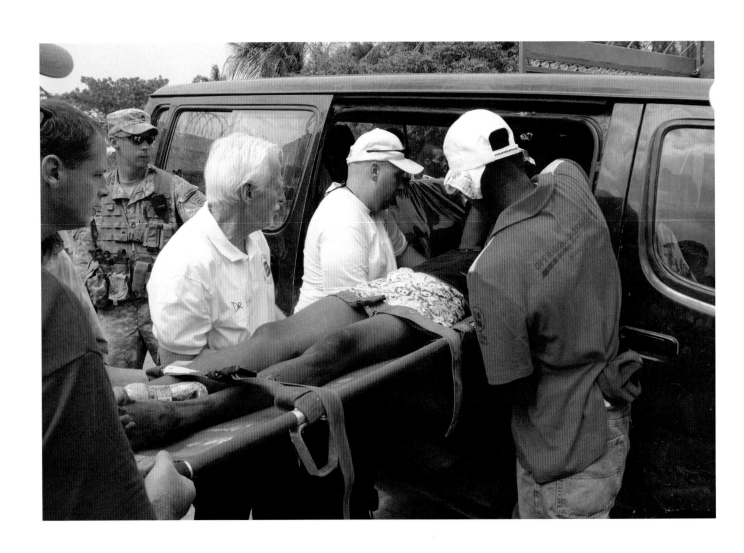

(Above) Haitian Armel Deye holds a picture of her missing daughter Fabiola Deye in front of a collapsed market. (Opposite page) Salvation Army and other relief personnel load an injured woman into a van for transport to a medical facility.

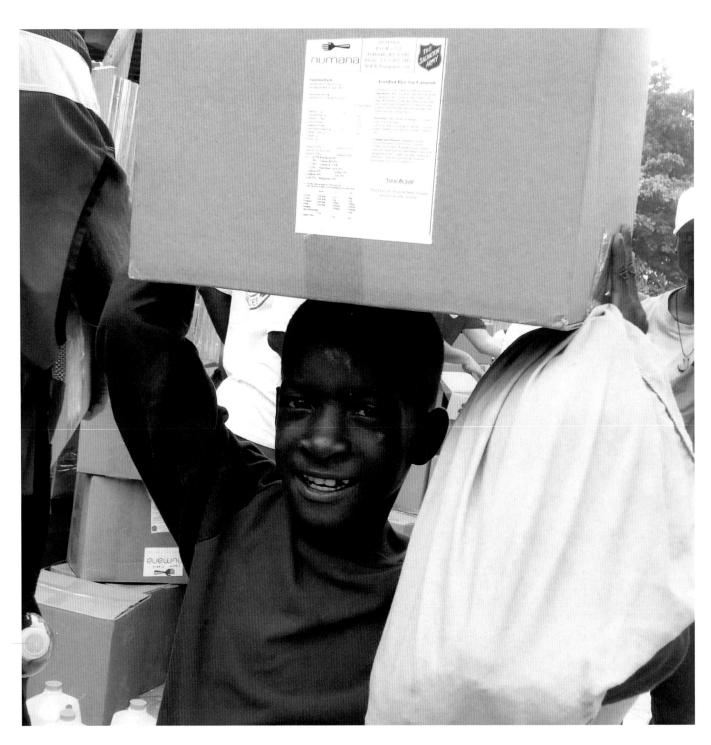

(Above) A boy carries a box of food provided by Numana and distributed by the Salvation Army. (Opposite page) A U.S. Army soldier carries an injured child from a helicopter as she is brought in for care after being hurt during the massive earthquake.

Weeping may endure for a night, but joy

cometh in the morning.

Psalm 30:5

"The European Union is committed to Haiti, a country with which Europeans have many links. After the disaster, the EU and its Member States responded quickly, in coordination with international partners, in order to alleviate suffering and restore minimum conditions for the population."

Herman Van Rompuy, president of the EU's European Council

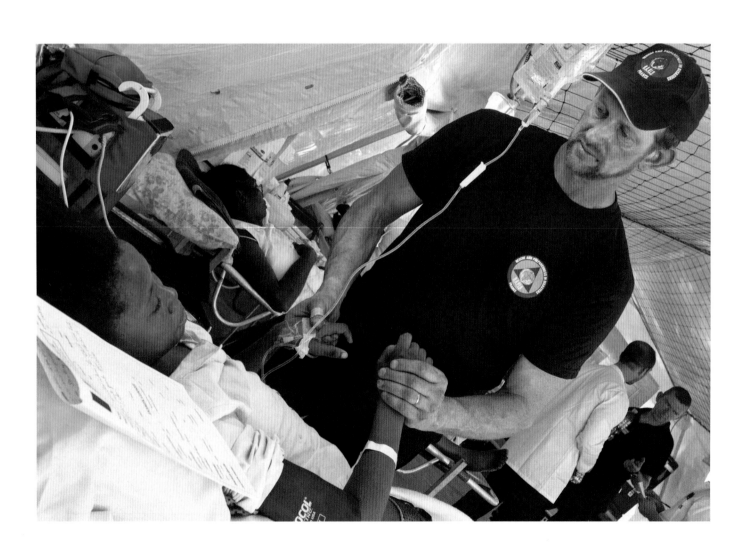

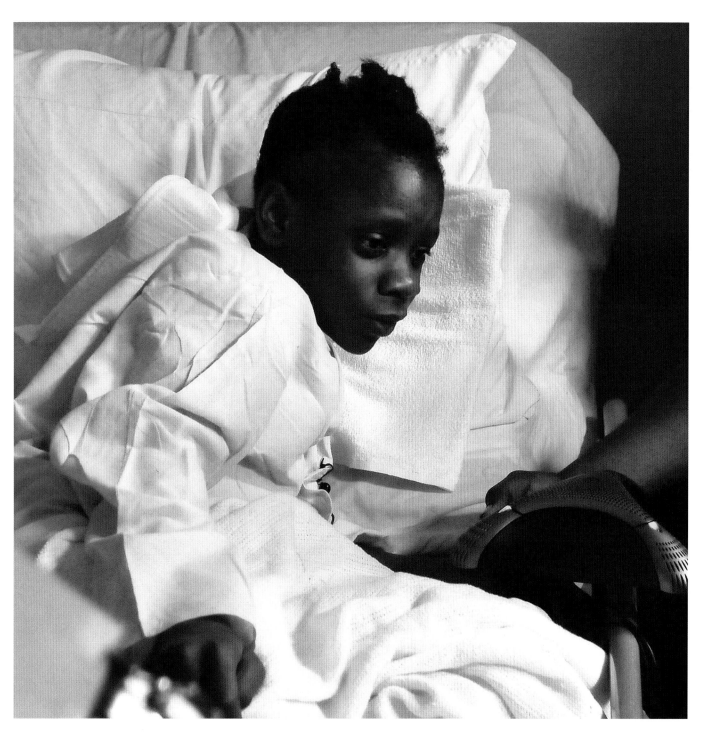

(Above) A 12-year-old patient aboard the Nimitz-class aircraft carrier USS Carl Vinson speaks with family members over a speakerphone two days after she was flown aboard to have a piece of concrete removed from her skull. (Opposite page) A French Civil Security member takes care of a Haitian patient in a field hospital set up at the site of the French Lycee (high school) in the Haitian capital.

(Above) A U.S. Air Force C-17 Globemaster III airdrops humanitarian aid into the outskirts of Port-au-Prince. (Opposite page) A U.S. Army Ranger stands guard over supplies being prepped for distribution.

"After Sept. 11, the way the world reached out to us, we have an obligation now. Even if Haiti didn't send anything monetarily in 2001, I'm sure they sent their prayers to us and it's our turn now."

James Cole, New York City police detective
and rescue team member

He only is my rock and my salvation: he is my defence; I shall not be moved. In God is my salvation and my glory: the rock of my strength, and my refuge, is in God.

Psalm 62:6-7

(Above) Haiti's ambassador to the United States, Raymond Joseph, holds a candle at vigil outside the Haitian embassy in Washington, D.C. (Opposite page) People pass by a destroyed house with a large bed still standing on the devastated second floor.

(Above) A baby sleeps peacefully during the aftermath of the earthquake.
(Opposite page) Haitian women gather supplies from the ruins of several buildings.

❝I appeal to the generosity of all to ensure our concrete

solidarity and the effective support of the international community

for these brothers and sisters who are living a time of need

and suffering.**❞**

Pope Benedict XVI

"I know I picked the Brahms, the Franz, the Sibelius. I picked several. I know a lot of concertos for violins. And I picked the longer ones."

Blind violinist Romel Joseph, who imagined violin concertos while buried for 18 hours in rubble

(Above) Haitian citizens, such as this man breaking up rubble, have been a major part of the relief and cleanup efforts. (Opposite page) Haitian men hold simple tools they are using to get into the rubble of a building.

(Above) MINUSTAH's Jordanian Battalion set up and opened a 12-bed hospital at their base. The peacekeepers are feeding any children that enter and are treating patients. (Opposite page) A U.S. Navy helicopter lands next to troops in front of the heavily damaged presidential palace.

"It's not an exaggeration to say that 10 years of hard work — at least — awaits the world in Haiti. We must hold ourselves and each other accountable for the commitments we make."

Canadian Prime Minister Stephen Harper

"We're on course to regain control. The aid is being organized and (the situation) will continue to improve."

Haitian President Rene Preval

(Above) An aerial view of the destroyed cathedral taken one week after the quake. (Opposite page) Seen through the fence surrounding the grounds, the Presidential Palace lies in ruins.

(Above) A Haitian child drinks a nutritional beverage at an aid station specifically for children. (Opposite page) Haitians sit on the Place St. Pierre, where about 1,000 people were living.

" Today, Mexico is present, in solidarity with Haiti, and we will make every effort to help the Haitian people. **"**

Mexican President Felipe Calderón

"We will make utmost efforts to help save the lives of people in Haiti in cooperation with other countries worldwide.**"**

Japanese Prime Minister Yukio Hatoyama

(Above) Miche Guerieri, 21, sits on a boat with her six-week-old baby after spending three days on a crowded ship off the coast of Port-au-Prince. (Opposite page) Locals sail on boats to reach and board a ship to Jeremie, about 200 kilometers (130 miles) from Port-au-Prince.

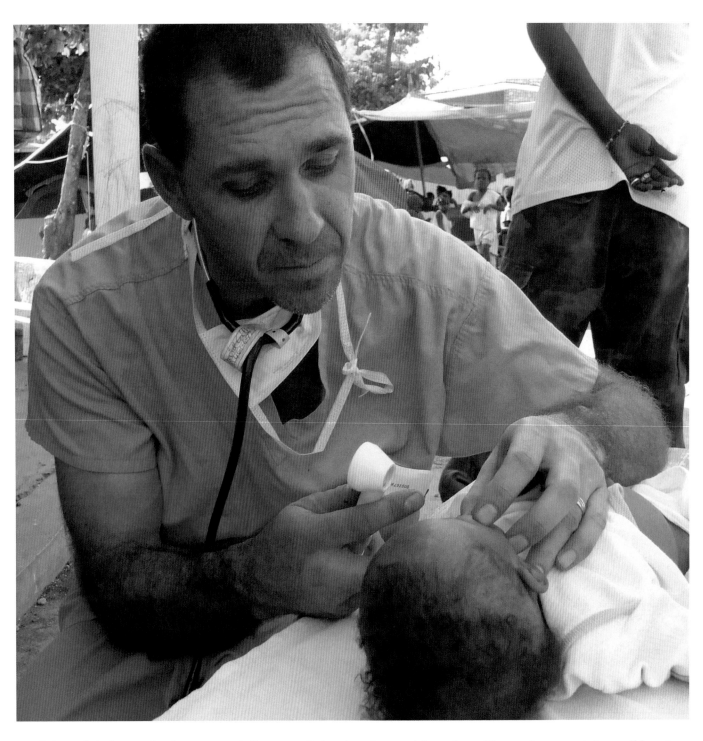

(Above) A doctor looks over an infant at a Salvation Army aid station. (Opposite page) A small boat pilots in front of the USNS Comfort, a floating medical treatment facility in the harbor.

❝Our nation is in distress, but we have a merciful Father. Our load is so, so heavy on our shoulders. Open the door so we can go and help, serve and heal.**❞**

Rev. Jacques Dumornay, pastor of First Haitian Baptist Church of Pompano Beach, Florida

"This is a huge undertaking and a long-term battle, and the world must focus on rescue, relief and reconstruction for Haiti.**"**

Rev. Jesse Jackson

(Above) U.S. Rev. Jesse Jackson stares at devastated buildings in Port-au-Prince.
(Opposite page) Women walk past the ruins of several buildings in Port-au-Prince.

(Above) A Haitian child sits in silence. (Opposite page) U.S. soldiers carry an injured Haitian to a helicopter at the Haitian Presidential Palace yard.

"I just cried and ran to my baby. I just could not believe she had been spared or that one so new to life, with so little strength, could have survived the collapsing walls with no injury at all."

Michel Joassaint, upon learning her 3-week-old baby, Elisabeth, had survived

At the core of every religion is the belief that we care for one another, we take care of each other especially in times of need. The Haitian people need our help, they need to know they're not alone, they need to know that we still care."

Actor George Clooney

(Above) Haitian earthquake survivors build a house in Brachs. (Opposite page) Citizens pull a cart full of salvaged wood, which will most likely be used to build temporary shelters.

(Above) Many Haitians are now living in tent cities like this one.
(Opposite page) These temporary living quarters are sprawled throughout Port-au-Prince.

"Our minds and hearts are with the Haitian people and we pray for them to surpass this difficult moment."

Honduran President-elect Porfirio Lobo

"I had an app that had pre-downloaded all this information about treating wounds. So I looked up excessive bleeding and I looked up compound fracture. So I knew I wasn't making mistakes. That gave me confidence to treat my wounds properly.**"**

Aid worker Dan Woolley

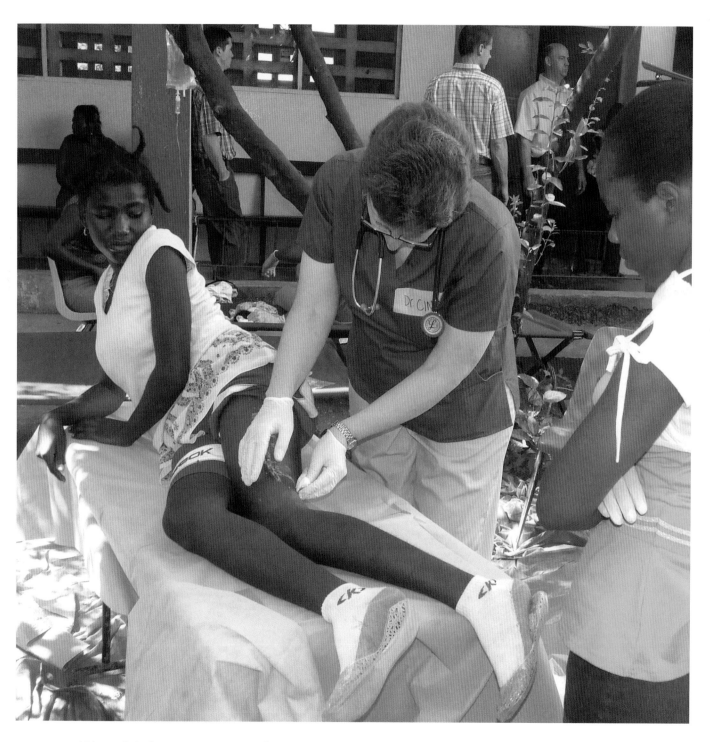

(Above) A doctor treats a gash on a Haitian girl's leg. (Opposite page) Doctors receive instructions on treating patients in Port-au-Prince.

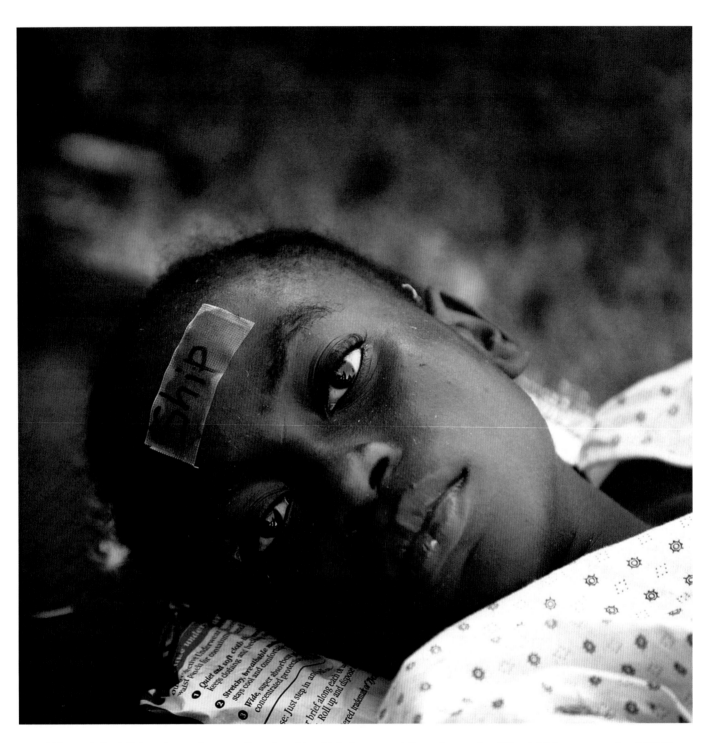

(Above) A child waits to be medivack ed by U.S. Army soldiers from the 82nd Airborne to the USNS Comfort. (Opposite page) An MH-60S helicopter lands on board the USNS Comfort, a U.S. Naval hospital ship, with Haitian earthquake victims needing medical treatment.

"I spent seven grueling days surrounded by endless images of despair and destruction. Then I witnessed a miracle. Kiki's smile will live with me forever.**"**

New York Post photographer Matthew McDermott, about a child being reunited with his mother

"We are in belief that the Haitian people, under the leadership of their government, will overcome difficulties and rebuild their homes at an early date with the help of the international community."

Chinese Foreign Ministry spokeswoman Jiang Yu

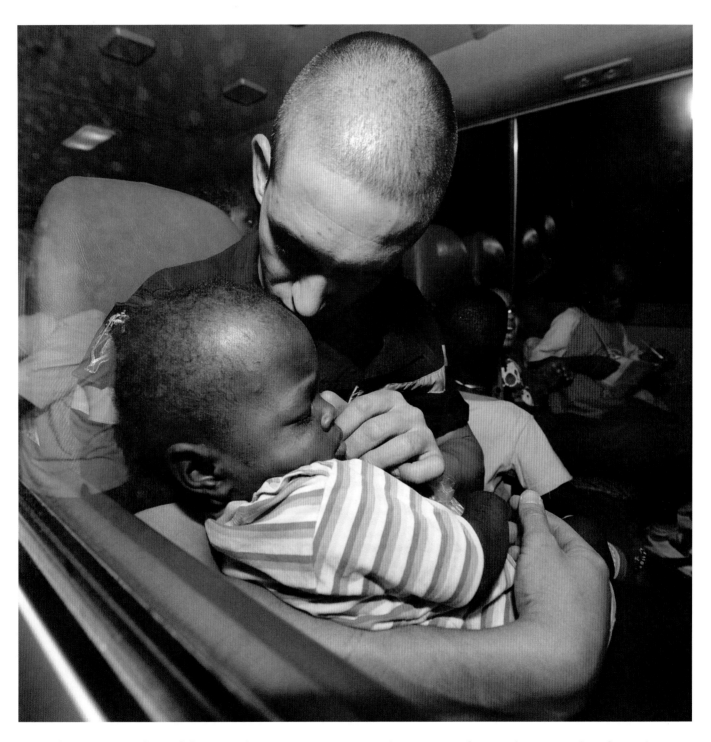

(Above) A member of the French emergency services kisses one of 33 orphans on a bus from the Lycee Francais in Port-au-Prince on their way to the airport to be flown to France for adoption. (Opposite page) A doctor smiles as Haitian children gather around him.

(Above) Salvation Army and U.S. Army members supervise a line of Haitians waiting for supplies. (Opposite page) Salvation Army personnel ready food and water to be distributed to the waiting masses.

"It's a little miracle. She's one tough cookie.

She is indestructible. "

Reinhard Riedl, upon hearing his wife,
Nadine Cardoso, had been rescued

❝We come together to support our friends, the Haitian people, as they seek a better future for a country that has already suffered more than we can imagine.**❞**

Canadian Foreign Affairs Minister Lawrence Cannon

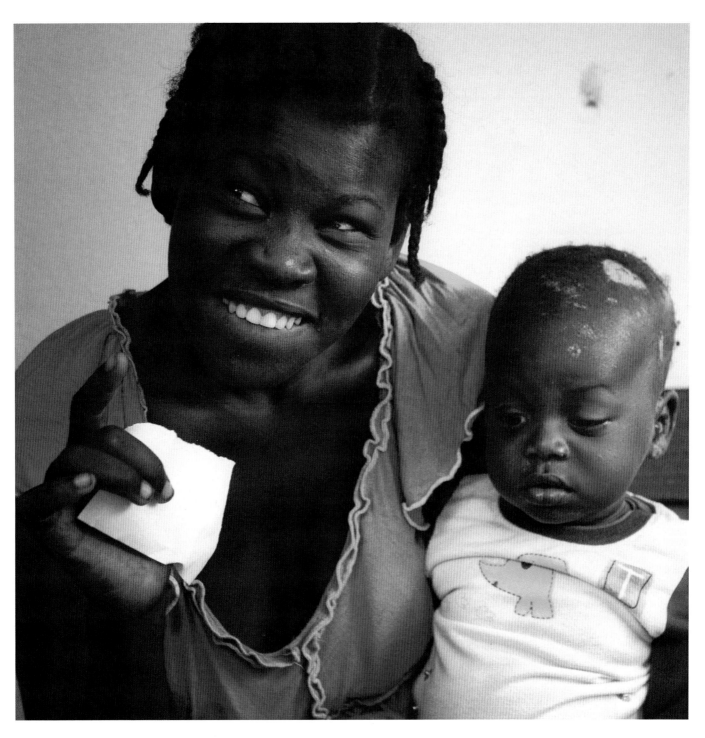

(Above) A mother smiles as she holds her child, injured but alive. (Opposite page) A woman near her tent on January 22, 2010, in Port-au-Prince.

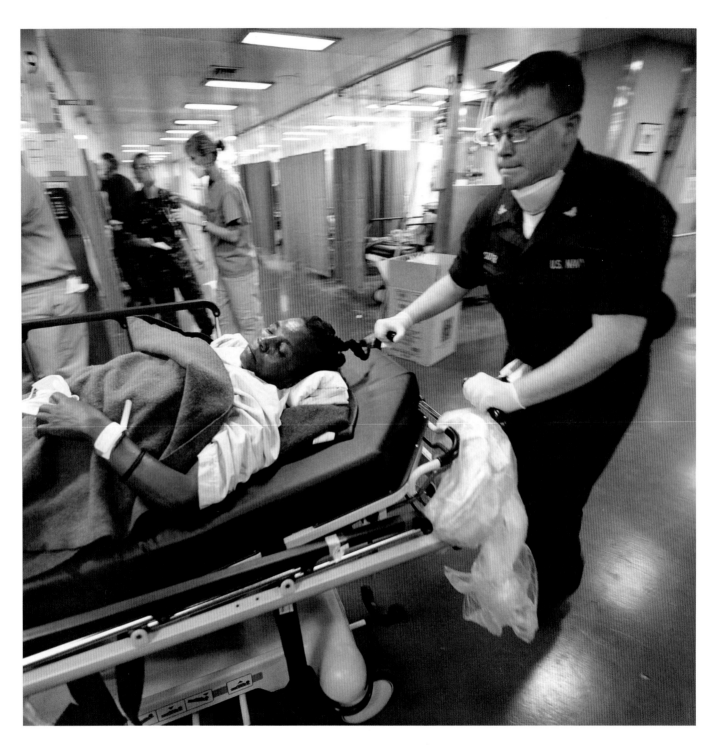

(Above) A Haitian earthquake victim is transported through a ward aboard the USNS Comfort hospital ship. (Opposite page) The USNS Comfort hospital ship anchored off the coast of Port-au-Prince on January 22, 2010. The Comfort arrived to give lifesaving care following the January 12 earthquake.

"It's a big miracle for me. When I leave the hospital I will give my heart to the Lord because he saved my life."

Wismond Exantus Jean Pierre, rescued after 11 days

For he shall give his angels charge over thee, to keep

thee in all thy ways.

Psalm 91:11

(Above) A little girl smiles as she receives a hug from a Salvation Army worker.
(Opposite page) Haitian babies rest on mattresses inside an aid station specifically for infants.

(Above) A member of a French rescue team helps carry a man found alive who had been trapped for 11 days in the rubble of a collapsed restaurant in downtown Port-au-Prince. (Opposite page) A member of a French rescue team works to free a man trapped in the rubble of a collapsed restaurant.

" This is God. "

Frank Louvier, the chief of the French rescue team who found a buried man alive 11 days after the earthquake.

God is our refuge and strength, a very present

help in trouble.

Psalm 46:1

(Above) A Salvation Army worker hands a woman a jug of drinking water. (Opposite page) A U.N. peacekeeper from Sri Lanka supervises a line of Haitians waiting for supplies from the Salvation Army.

(Above) U.N. peacekeepers watch over Salvation Army personnel distributing supplies in Petit Goave, nearly 60 miles west of Port-au-Prince. (Opposite page) A man brushes his teeth at a makeshift camp.

"It truly is a miracle, she came back to life bit by bit.

She is blessed by the gods."

Surgeon Dominique Jean, on an 11-year-old
girl rescued from rubble

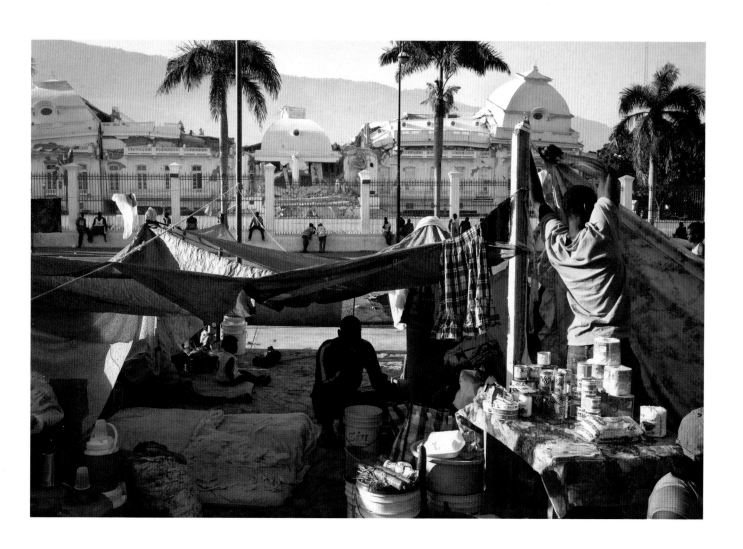

"Frank actually literally lifted her out of the wreckage. Just like the cavalry. You can't script that stuff. **"**

Clay Cook, whose daughter Jillian was
rescued by her husband

(Above) A woman is comforted by a priest after the funeral of Haitian Archbishop Joseph Serge Miot, killed in the devastating earthquake outside Notre Dame d'Assumption Cathedral. (Opposite page) Haitian President Rene Preval (center) is greeted by U.S. Archbishop Timothy Dolan (left) before the funeral of Haitian Archbishop Joseph Serge Miot.

(Above) Though her country lies in ruins, this little girl's smile speaks to her spirit, and the spirit of the entire Haitian community. (Opposite page) Haitians take part in an open-air mass at Jean-Jacques.

"My baby is alive. I know that God is watching over us now.**"**

Marie Yolène Bois de Fer, 46, clothing vendor

And he took the children in his arms, put his hands on them and blessed them.

Mark 10:16

Photo Credits